THE MAN WHO BOUGHT AMERICA

WRITER: Ed Brubaker

Penciler, Issues #37-38 & #40-42:
Steve Epting with **Luke Ross** (Issue #42)
Inkers, #37-38 & #40-42:
Steve Epting, Mike Perkins, Rick Magyar
& Fabio Laguna
Artist, Issue #39: Roberto De La Torre
Colorist: Frank D'Armata
Letterer: VC's Joe Caramagna

Cover Art: Steve Epting
Associate Editors:
Molly Lazer & Jeanine Schaefer
Editor: Tom Brevoort

New Captain America costume
design by Alex Ross
Captain America created by
Joe Simon & Jack Kirby

Collection Editor: Jennifer Grünwald
Editorial Assistant: Alex Starbuck
Assistant Editors: Cory Levine & John Denning
Editor, Special Projects: Mark D. Beazley
Senior Editor, Special Projects: Jeff Youngquist
Senior Vice President of Sales: David Gabriel

Production: Jerron Quality Color
& Jerry Kalinowski
Vice President of Creative: Tom Marvelli

Editor in Chief: Joe Quesada
Publisher: Dan Buckley

Previously:

The Red Skull, with the help of megalomaniacal psychiatrist Dr. Faustus, manipulated Sharon Carter, former Agent 13 of S.H.I.E.L.D., into taking the life of Steve Rogers, the man who was Captain America. Now pregnant with Steve Rogers' baby, Sharon is held prisoner, both physically and mentally, by her enemies.

Cap's former partner James "Bucky" Barnes has agreed to don the mantle of Captain America and go after the Red Skull. However, Aleksander Lukin, the ex-Soviet General whose mind the Red Skull has secretly been sharing, faked his death in a plane crash. Meanwhile, Lukas's Kronas Corporation is making moves that rock the American economy and the Red Skull has set up his own politician to further his political agenda.

And, while looking around in the Red Skull's base, Sharon Carter has stumbled upon a figure that looks very much like the deceased Steve Rogers...

CAPTAIN AMERICA: THE DEATH OF CAPTAIN AMERICA VOL. 3 — THE MAN WHO BOUGHT AMERICA. Contains material originally published in magazine form as CAPTAIN AMERICA #37-42. First printing 2008. Hardcover ISBN# 978-0-7851-2970-7. Softcover ISBN# 978-0-7851-2971-4. Published by MARVEL PUBLISHING, INC., a subsidiary of MARVEL ENTERTAINMENT, INC. OFFICE OF PUBLICATION: 417 5th Avenue, New York, NY 10016. Copyright © 2008 Marvel Characters, Inc. All rights reserved. Hardcover: $19.99 per copy in the U.S. and $21.00 in Canada (GST #R127032852). Softcover: $14.99 per copy in the U.S. and $15.75 in Canada (GST #R127032852). Canadian Agreement #40668537. All characters featured in this issue and the distinctive names and likenesses thereof, and all related indicia are trademarks of Marvel Characters, Inc. No similarity between any of the names, characters, persons, and/or institutions in this magazine with those of any living or dead person or institution is intended, and any such similarity which may exist is purely coincidental. **Printed in the U.S.A.** ALAN FINE, CEO Marvel Toys & Publishing Divisions and CMO Marvel Characters, Inc.; DAVID GABRIEL, SVP of Publishing Sales & Circulation; DAVID BOGART, SVP of Business Affairs & Talent Management; MICHAEL PASCIULLO, VP of Merchandising & Communications; JIM O'KEEFE, VP of Operations & Logistics; DAN CARR, Executive Director of Publishing Technology; JUSTIN F. GABRIE, Director of Editorial Operations; SUSAN CRESPI, Editorial Operations Manager; OMAR OTIEKU, Production Manager; STAN LEE, Chairman Emeritus. For information regarding advertising in Marvel Comics or on Marvel.com, please contact Mitch Dane,

Paris, France.
August – 1944

‹LOOK AT THEM...JUST LOOK...›

‹THE LIBERATORS OF EUROPE... MARCHING IN LIKE FOOLS...›

‹THE SMUGNESS OF AMERICANS DISGUSTS ME...›

‹THESE LITTLE CHILDREN OF THE WORLD... SO FULL OF UNDESERVING PRIDE...›

AND JUST YESTERDAY, IT WAS SENATOR WRIGHT WHO NEGOTIATED WITH **KRONAS ENERGY** TO LOWER THE PRICE OF OIL BACK TO PRE-CRISIS LEVELS...

KANE-MEYER STOPS RIOT IN WASHINGTON — 5:23 p ES

...AND TO HALT THE FORECLOSURE OF THOUSANDS OF HOMES AROUND THE COUNTRY.

I ALMOST CAN'T BELIEVE THIS IS WORKING...

KRONAS REDUCES PRICE OF OIL — 5:23 p ES

...BUT HAVING **YOUR OWN** MINIONS PUBLICLY ATTACK THE SENATOR SHOULD SQUASH ANY ACCUSATIONS THAT HE'S YOUR MAN...

...OR THAT THE **RED SKULL** IS SECRETLY RUNNING KRONAS INTERNATIONAL.

YES... ALTHOUGH I SUPPOSE LUKIN DOES DESERVE **SOME** OF THE CREDIT...

...IF HE'D EVER STOP **COMPLAINING** ABOUT THE RESULTS.

I SIMPLY PREFER TO DESTROY THIS PLACE FROM THE **INSIDE OUT.**

IT'S MORE **SATISFYING**, AFTER ALL, TO TAKE TIME WITH YOUR PREY.

I COULDN'T AGREE MORE.

NOW OUR MAN CAN RUN AS THE *OUTSIDER* WHO *SAVED* HIS COUNTRY FROM RUIN...

AND SLOWLY, HE'LL SHOW THEM THAT A *POLICE STATE* IS THE ONLY ANSWER TO THE CHAOS OF DEMOCRACY.

SOON *KANE-MEYER SECURITIES* WILL BE PROTECTING *EVERY CITY* IN THIS NATION...

MY HAND WILL WRAP AROUND THE THROAT OF THE WHOLE UNITED STATES.

YOU MEAN, *OUR HAND,* I BELIEVE.

DON'T YOU HAVE SOMETHING *ELSE* TO DO, FAUSTUS?

A WOMAN CARRYING A *BABY* THAT SHE KEPT *SECRET* FROM YOU, PERHAPS?

AGENT 13 WILL *KEEP...* I THOUGHT YOU WANTED TO DISCUSS OUR *NEW* PATIENT.

OR IS ZOLA STILL FIGURING OUT HOW TO *AWAKEN* HIM?

NO, EVERYTHING IS ON SCHEDULE.

HE'LL BE CONSCIOUS SOON, AND THEN IT WON'T JUST BE THIS *STRIPLING* WEARING THE FLAG.

IS THERE A NEW CAPTAIN AMERICA?

5:23

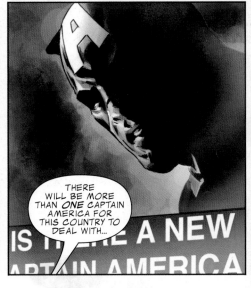

THERE WILL BE MORE THAN *ONE* CAPTAIN AMERICA FOR THIS COUNTRY TO DEAL WITH...

IS THERE A NEW CAPTAIN AMERICA

--STILL NO OFFICIAL COMMENT ON THE APPEARANCE OF A MAN IN A CAPTAIN AMERICA UNIFORM AT THE RIOTS IN D.C....

GOT ME CHASING DOWN LEADS, TRYING TO TRACK SHARON...

...WHILE YOU'RE GOING BEHIND MY BACK-- WITH THIS?!

SAM, IT'S NOT LIKE THAT...

OH, IT'S NOT, HUNH?

'CAUSE THIS WOULDN'T BE THE FIRST TIME YOU MADE A UNILATERAL DECISION THAT AFFECTS US ALL.

I AM TRYING TO FOLLOW STEVE'S WISHES, OKAY?

HE WANTED BUCKY SAVED... AND HE WANTED CAPTAIN AMERICA TO GO ON.

SO YOU JUST DECIDED TO KILL TWO BIRDS WITH ONE STONE?

IN A MANNER OF SPEAKING...BUT THAT ISN'T HOW I MEANT IT.

"...I'M NOT THE ONLY ONE WHO'S GONNA DISAPPROVE..."

ALL RIGHT, BUCK...TIGHTEN IT UP.

DON'T JUST LET YOUR ARM DO ALL THE MECHANICS.

DO THE MATH BEFORE YOU RELEASE.

LEARN THE ANGLES, LEARN THE WEIGHT.

MAKE IT INSTINCTIVE.

BECAUSE YOU DON'T WANNA BE CHASING THIS DAMN THING DOWN IN THE MIDDLE OF A FIGHT.

NOT WHEN YOU...

HEY--

GGANKK

YOU **REALLY** WANT TO DROP THAT SHIELD RIGHT NOW.

HEY, THAT'S KINDA **FUNNY**... I WAS JUST ABOUT TO SAY THE **SAME THING** TO YOU.

I MEAN, SAM TOLD ME YOU WERE **ALIVE**... AND I WOULDN'T EXACTLY SAY I WAS **SURPRISED**...NOT IN **OUR** WORLD.

BUT I NEVER THOUGHT YOU'D BE **STUPID** ENOUGH TO TRY TO WEAR HIS MASK.

THE SHIELD, **BARTON**. I'M SERIOUS.

SO, YOU **KNOW** WHO I AM?

YEAH. YOU **USED** TO BE HAWKEYE.

THEN YOU HAD TO KNOW IT WAS ONLY A MATTER OF TIME BEFORE I SHOWED UP TO KICK YOUR @##.

ACTUALLY, IT DIDN'T EVEN *CROSS* MY MIND.

WHERE *I'M* FROM, THE GOOD GUYS FOUGHT ON THE *SAME* SIDE...

THEY DIDN'T JUST START *THROWING* PUNCHES AT EACH OTHER.

SMATT

HUNH...

YEAH, HE TAUGHT *ME* THAT MOVE, TOO.

NOW, IF YOU WANNA *TALK*, I'M FINE WITH THAT.

BUT I *DON'T* HAVE TO EXPLAIN MY ACTIONS TO YOU.

I DON'T KNOW HOW IT'S POSSIBLE, BUT... HE'S ALIVE.

STEVE IS ALIVE.

HE'S ALIVE AND HE'S HERE.

SO I CAN'T LEAVE YET...NOT WITHOUT HIM.

AGENT 13?

I JUST HAVE TO PRETEND I HAVEN'T BROKEN FREE... AND PLAY ALONG.

YES, DOCTOR?

YOUR PRESENCE IS NOT REQUIRED FOR THIS.

RETURN TO YOUR QUARTERS.

YES, DOCTOR.

AH, FAUSTUS... GOOD OF YOU TO JOIN US...

IS THAT A *JOKE*, ZOLA? BECAUSE YOU WOULDN'T EVEN *HAVE* THAT PATIENT IF NOT FOR ME.

LEVEL 07

BUT SOON... TONIGHT.

ONCE HE'S AWAKE... MOBILE...

THEN WE'RE ALL GETTING OUT OF HERE.

ALREADY BUSTED SOME *RIBS*, HUNH?

MAN... I *REALLY* NEED TO UPGRADE THIS PLACE'S SECURITY SYSTEM.

YOU LEFT THE LIGHTS ON DOWNSTAIRS... I THOUGHT YOU WERE *TRAINING*.

YOU AREN'T HERE TO *FIGHT*, I HOPE?

FIGHT?

NEVER MIND... STUPID QUESTION.

SO WHAT *ARE* YOU DOING HERE?

WELL, I SAW THE NEWS... SAW *YOU* ON THE NEWS.

I GUESSED *THAT* MUCH.

AND WHILE I'M FAR FROM *THRILLED*...

I FIGURE *SOMEONE* NEEDS TO MAKE SURE YOU DON'T GET YOURSELF KILLED.

WAIT...YOU WANNA *WORK* TOGETHER?

I'VE GOT A *LEAD* ON TRACKING DOWN SHARON, MAYBE... SO YEAH...

I'M FIGURING MAYBE YOU AN' ME GO TRY AND SAVE MY FRIEND.

AND I CAN SEE IF YOU'RE REALLY *WORTHY* OF CARRYING THAT SHIELD.

UNLESS YOU'RE TOO INJURED?

NAH, I'VE BEEN HURT WORSE THAN *THIS* LOTS OF TIMES... I'M A QUICK HEALER.

SO, WHAT DO YOU SAY?

I SAY, LET'S GO SAVE THE GIRL.

OKAY, SHARON...LET'S DO THIS.

SECURITY CAMERAS DISABLED...

ALARM CODES NEUTRALIZED...

ACCESS GRANTED...

LET'S GO SAVE OUR MAN.

STEVE...?
CAN YOU...

CAN YOU HEAR ME?

...WHAT...?
WHO...WHO'S THERE...?

OH MY GOD... NO.

YOU'RE NOT--

YOU'RE NOT STEVE.

WAIT... YES...

STEVE... STEVE ROGERS... YES.

THAT *WAS* MY NAME...

BUT... WHO ARE *YOU*?

BECAUSE YEARS AGO, DR. FAUSTUS MADE HIM SET HIMSELF *ON FIRE*... THAT'S HOW I KNOW WHO HE IS. FROM THE SCARS.

THE *GRAND DIRECTOR.*

WHO WAS *ALSO* THE CAPTAIN AMERICA OF THE *NINETEEN-FIFTIES.*

I LIKE IKE

A GUY WHO HAD EVERYTHING ABOUT HIMSELF ALTERED SO HE COULD BE JUST LIKE THE REAL STEVE ROGERS...

HE EVEN DISCOVERED A VERSION OF THE SUPER-SOLDIER SERUM AND USED IT ON HIMSELF AND *HIS* BUCKY-- JACK MONROE.

UNFORTUNATELY, THE *SERUM* HE AND JACK TOOK BACK THEN WAS *INCOMPLETE*, AND IT *TWISTED* THEIR MINDS...

TAKE THAT, *COMMIE!*

MADE THEM START TO SEE AMERICA'S *ENEMIES* EVERYWHERE.

AND WHEN FAUSTUS GOT HOLD OF THEM DECADES LATER, HE TRIED TO USE THEM TO RIP THIS COUNTRY APART ALONG THE *RACIAL DIVIDE.*

BUT STEVE STOPPED HIM.

LIKE HE ALWAYS DID.

JACK MANAGED TO SURVIVE THE EXPERIENCE, AND EVENTUALLY WENT ON TO BECOME *NOMAD*...

AND TO BECOME ONE OF *MY* STEVE'S BEST FRIENDS...

BUT NOW, JACK'S DEAD... AND SO IS STEVE...

YET SOMEHOW, THIS *ABOMINATION* IS STILL ALIVE.

PLEASE... WHY WON'T YOU JUST *TALK* TO ME...?

I KNOW I'VE SEEN YOU BEFORE...

IT'S A SICK JOKE, BUT SO ARE *ALL* THE RED SKULL'S JOKES. SO WHY DOES *THIS ONE* SEEM WORSE?

BECAUSE HE'S WEARING MY DEAD LOVER'S FACE?

I CAN'T LET THIS GO ON.

HEY--HEY, WHAT'RE YOU--

--DON'T DO THAT!

I'M SORRY... I REALLY AM.

AAAIIEEE!

ZZZAAAPTT

IT SEEMS YOUR PATIENT ISN'T EXACTLY *YOUR* PATIENT ANYMORE, DR. FAUSTUS.

AND YOUR GRASP OF THE *OBVIOUS* IS IMPRESSIVE, LUKIN.

THIS WOULDN'T HAVE HAPPENED AT ALL IF ZOLA HAD BEEN HERE MONITORING THE SUBJECT.

DON'T TRY AND *ADJUST* THE BLAME.

I'M NOT...

...BUT WE HAVE OTHER MATTERS TO TEND TO.

SHE... SHE WAS GOING TO *KILL ME...*

THERE, THERE, MY BOY...SHE WAS JUST *CONFUSED...*

NOW LET'S GET YOU BACK TO BED.

SHE... SHE KNEW MY NAME, TOO...

OF *COURSE* SHE DID.

EVERYONE KNOWS YOU...

YOU'RE *CAPTAIN AMERICA.*

HE'S LIKE AN INFANT, FAUSTUS.

HE'LL BE FINE. HE'S JUST DISORIENTED. HE'S BEEN SLEEPING A LONG TIME.

BUT HIS BODY HEALED WELL OVER THOSE YEARS.

AS I *SUSPECTED* IT WOULD.

WELL, FOR YOUR SAKE...I HOPE YOUR WORK WITH *HIM* WILL BE MORE EFFECTIVE THAN IT WAS WITH *AGENT 13.*

HEY, FALCON...YOU *SURE* THERE'S SOMETHING UP THIS WAY?

WE'VE BEEN ON THE ROAD FOR *HOURS*...

S.H.I.E.L.D. *SATELLITES* SHOWED TRUCKS GOIN' NORTHEAST ON THIS ROAD, FROM THE FACILITY WHERE *FAUSTUS* AND HIS PEOPLE WERE.

IT'S THE BEST LEAD WE'VE GOT.

HELL, IT'S THE *ONLY* LEAD WE'VE GOT.

ANY IDEA WHAT IT *WAS* THEY LOADED INTO THOSE TRUCKS?

NAH, THE FIELD TEAM SWEPT THE PLACE I FOUND AND CAME UP EMPTY.

ONLY THING WE KNOW IS IT USED TO BE A *HIGH-END MENTAL CLINIC* THAT FAUSTUS WAS RUNNING AS A *FRONT*.

SO IT'S SOMETHING HE WAS *SITTING* ON FOR A LONG TIME...

AND THAT COULD BE ALL KINDS OF NASTINESS.

I KNOW... I'VE *MET* THE MAN, REMEMBER?

WELL, REMIND ME TO TELL YOU ABOUT THE **RACE WAR** HE TRIED TO START BACK IN THE DAY...

OH, *HOLD UP--* STOP OVER TO THE RIGHT, IN THAT *COVER.*

WE'RE HERE.

WHERE?

WHERE THE TRUCKS STOPPED.

SOME OLD FACTORY...

OKAY, LET'S CHECK IT.

HOLD UP...LET'S GET SOME RECON FIRST.

I KNOW HOW TO *RECON,* SAM.

NOT AS GOOD AS *REDWING,* YOU DON'T.

DOES YOUR BIRD *TALK?*

JUST TO ME... AND IT'S NOT EXACTLY *TALKING.*

I CAN *SEE* WHAT HE SEES.

SO, WHAT'S HE SEEING?

A.I.M. AGENTS... LOOKS LIKE THEY'RE SHUTTING THIS PLACE DOWN.

AND SOMETHING ELSE...

OH YEAH... WE'VE GOT ONE OF THE SKULL'S *BIG GUNS* HERE.

PROFESSOR ARNIM ZOLA HIMSELF IS OVERSEEING THIS CLEANUP.

THAT'S THE *SCIENTIST?* THE ROBOT GUY?

YEAH... AND IF HE'S *HERE*, THAT MEANS THIS PLACE IS IMPORTANT.

WELL THEN, IT LOOKS LIKE THE RED SKULL'S ABOUT TO BE BACK WHERE I LIKE HIM...

ON THE LOSING SIDE OF THE BATTLE.

--AND THIS BATTLE WILL NOT BE WON DOING THINGS *THE OLD WAY!*

THE POLITICS OF THE PAST, THE POLITICS OF CORRUPTION AND DEGRADATION HAVE LED US TO THIS PLACE!

A PLACE WHERE OUR ECONOMY STANDS ON THE VERGE OF ANOTHER GREAT DEPRESSION!

WING FOR A NEW AMERICA

WRIGHT FOR AMERICA

WHERE OUR CITIZENS ARE AFRAID TO WALK THEIR OWN STREETS AT NIGHT!

AND I SAY NO MORE! IT'S TIME FOR THE RULE OF LAW TO RETAKE AMERICA!

THE RIGHT WING AND THE LEFT WING HAVE GOTTEN US TO THIS STALEMATE! IT'S TIME FOR A NEW WING, A THIRD WING-- TO UNITE US ALL!

SENATOR GORDON WRIGHT, GIVING A *MAJOR* SPEECH ON HIS THIRD PARTY CANDIDACY FOR *PRESIDENT* TODAY...

★ FOR ★

SEN. WRIGHT GIVES FIRST MAJOR SPEECH

5:23 p ES

AND AS MOST REPORTS HAVE NOTED, HE DREW QUITE A CROWD.

AN ESTIMATED TEN THOUSAND PEOPLE CAME TO HEAR HIM SPEAK...

SEN. WRIGHT DRAWS 10K LISTENERS

5:23 p ES

AND EARLY POLLING SHOWS THAT IN JUST DAYS, THE SENATOR HAS *ALREADY* MADE WAVES IN THE CAMPAIGN... ALTHOUGH *SMALL* ONES.

EARLY POLLING RESULTS IN

5:23 p ES

OVER TWENTY PERCENT HAVE A *POSITIVE* VIEW OF THE SENATOR, AND WOULD *CONSIDER* VOTING FOR HIM IN NOVEMBER.

YES 20%

SEN. WRIGHT WELL LIKED POLLS SAY

5:23 p ES

BUT INDEPENDENTS PREFER HIM TO *ANY* OF THE DEMOCRATIC OR GOP CANDIDATES.

TWENTY PERCENT... THAT'S NOT GOING TO *DO* IT, SKULL.

THOSE ARE THE FIRST NUMBERS. THEY MEAN *NOTHING.*

AND THEY'LL MEAN *LESS* THAN NOTHING *SOON.*

I SUPPOSE... BUT LET'S NOT FORGET IT'LL BE *MY WORK* THAT MAKES IT SO.

YOU'RE NOT THE *ONLY ONE* IN THIS, SKULL... REMEMBER THAT.

I'M REMEMBERING THAT TIME ME AND CAP ALMOST CAUGHT THE RED SKULL NAPPING IN DENMARK AS FALCON AND I MOVE IN.

SOMETHING ABOUT SAM'S TONE, HIS MOOD...THE WAY HE CARRIES HIMSELF.

KRAKK

WHAT--?

IT DOESN'T REALLY REMIND ME OF STEVE... HE'S CLEARLY HIS OWN MAN.

BUT THERE'S SOMETHING THERE... SOMETHING I CAN'T PUT MY FINGER ON.

GET THEM!

SOMEONE ALERT DR. ZOLA!

AN INFLUENCE, I GUESS.

AND I HAVE TO ADMIT, IT MAKES ME SMILE.

WHAMM

KRAKK

THEN I REALIZE SOMETHING STRANGE...

NO PANICKING!

STOP THEM!

I CARE ABOUT NOT LETTING HIM DOWN.

SHOWING HIM I CAN DO THIS JOB.

THAT WHATEVER FAITH HE'S PUTTING IN ME ISN'T MISPLACED.

GUH-- AHHH!

GGYAAAAA!

THAT MUST BE WHY IT FEELS LIKE THE GOOD OLD DAYS.

MUCH AS I HATE TO *CALL* THEM THAT...

...TO REALIZE DEATH AND COMBAT ARE *THIS* COMFORTABLE TO ME.

BUT THEY ARE.

FALCON-- I'M GOING AFTER THE ROBOT!

THIS IS WHAT I WAS BORN FOR.

FOOL.

ZZAZZKKT

GYUHH—

YOU THINK ARNIM ZOLA FEARS YOU?!

THAT YOU ARE ANYTHING BUT A GNAT TO BE SQUASHED?!

HOLD THEM BACK! ALL OF YOU!

KRRRSSH

WATCH OUT!

I GOT THESE GUYS! DON'T LET ZOLA GET AWAY!

RIGHT-- YEAH!

SHUK

THEY THINK THEY'VE ACCOMPLISHED SOMETHING. FOOLS.

I'LL TAKE EVERYTHING IMPORTANT HERE WITH ME.

ZZUUKK

ZUUK

ZOOOP

THEY CAN HAVE THE VICTORY OF THE SCORCHED EARTH!

ENGAGE SEQUENCE

ENGAGE SEQUENCE

ALL RIGHT, ZOLA...STEP AWAY FROM THE--

SKKKRRRAAAKKKK

WHAT THE HELL?

TRU
IN
0:03

AW $#@%...

BUCKY!

--THE PEOPLE HAVE MISSED THEIR HERO...

AND THE COUNTRY NEEDS HIM, STEVEN... LIKE SHE'S *NEVER* NEEDED HIM BEFORE.

THEY NEED A MAN... A MAN OF *HONOR*...

TRULY *WORTHY* TO CARRY THE MANTLE OF *CAPTAIN AMERICA*.

ARE *YOU* THAT MAN?

I...

YES...

YES, I AM.

VVZZSSHHKKK

SKULL, I'M BACK FROM MY ERRAND. IT DID NOT GO AS PLANNED.

YOU'RE GOING TO WANT TO HEAR THIS RIGHT AWAY.

I HAVE TO GO...THERE'S BEEN SOME COMPLICATION.

LEAVE, THEN...I COULDN'T CARE LESS.

NOW THEN...LET US CONTINUE YOUR LESSONS.

YES, DOCTOR... PLEASE.

THIS MAN IS THE UNWORTHY COWARD...THE PRETENDER TO YOUR TITLE.

AND HE'S SOMETHING MUCH WORSE THAN THAT, MY CAPTAIN...

...HE'S ALSO THE MAN WHO KILLED JACK MONROE...

YOUR SIDEKICK.

BUCKY...?

"...I MEAN, THAT THING WASN'T ALL JUNK.

"THERE HAD TO BE SOME MEMORY CHIP OR SOMETHING...."

SOMETHING USEFUL. BUT WITH S.H.I.E.L.D. SPREAD SO THIN LIKE THEY'VE BEEN...

THEY'RE DOING THEIR BEST, BUCKY.

BUT ARNIM ZOLA IS A GENIUS ON THE DOCTOR DOOM LEVEL...

GETTING ANY CLUE OUT OF ONE OF HIS HALF-DESTROYED ROBOT BODIES ISN'T GONNA BE EASY.

NEVER MIND FINDING THE *EXACT CLUE* WE NEED TO LEAD US TO DR. FAUSTUS, THE RED SKULL...

...AND SHARON.

HEY--

I SHOULD'A *SEEN* THAT.

YOU WERE WORRYING TOO MUCH ABOUT THE METAL ARM.

YOU WOULD BE, TOO.

YEAH, I WOULD.

WE *HAVE* TO FIND HER, SAM...SHE *SAVED* ME FROM THEM.

DOES NO ONE REMEMBER ME *CATCHING* YOU?

ALL SHARON DID WAS THROW YOU *OUT OF A PLANE.*

BECAUSE SHE KNEW *YOU* WERE THERE...

SHE *HAD* TO.

AND THAT MEANS SHE *KNOWS,* SAM... SHE KNOWS WHO SHE REALLY IS, AND SHE'S *TRAPPED.*

IF SHE ISN'T ALREADY *DEAD* BY NOW.

NO...*NOT YET.* THAT'S NOT THE SKULL'S STYLE.

HE'LL WAIT TO KILL HER...'TIL WHEN IT'LL *HURT* THE MOST.

BREEET-DEEET

IT'S NATASHA.

BREEET-DEEET

HEY, 'TASHA...

WHAT? YEAH, I'M PRETTY SURE HE...

HOLD ON, WAIT. WE'RE DOWNSTAIRS... WHAT *CHANNEL?*

CAPTAIN AMERICA BACK

7:18 p ES

--IF YOU'RE JUST TUNING IN, OUR TOP STORY TONIGHT--HAS THE *REAL* CAPTAIN AMERICA RETURNED?

A DRAMATIC ENTRANCE

7:18 p ES

A STARTLING APPEARANCE BY A MAN WHO DRESSED AND SOUNDED REMARKABLY LIKE **STEVE ROGERS,** AMERICA'S SLAIN SUPER-SOLDIER, HAS THE MEDIA **ON FIRE** TONIGHT.

COULD THIS BE THE REAL THING?

7:18 p ES

COULD THIS BE THE REAL *CAPTAIN AMERICA?* BACK FROM THE DEAD?

THE OTHER CAP

7:18 p ES

AS MANY WILL RECALL, LAST WEEK SAW AN APPEARANCE OF ANOTHER MAN IN A CAPTAIN AMERICA SUIT, ALTHOUGH THAT WAS A VARIANT LOOK.

THWARTED ASSASSINATION ATTEMPT

7:18 p ES

BUT TONIGHT, CAPTAIN AMERICA LEAPT TO THE AID OF THIRD PARTY PRESIDENTIAL CANDIDATE WRIGHT...

WHO CAME UNDER ASSAULT BY RIGHT WING RADICALS DURING A SPEECH IN CHICAGO.

AND THEN, IN A BIZARRE TURN, THIS CAPTAIN AMERICA ADDRESSED THE CROWD, PRAISING SENATOR WRIGHT...

CAP ADDRESSES CROWD

7.19 p ES

BECAUSE NO ONE BUT THIS MAN HAS THE COURAGE TO DO WHAT MUST BE DONE...

...AISES SENATOR WRIGHT

7:19 p ES

...TO MAKE THE AMERICAN FUTURE THE DREAM IT WAS MEANT TO BE.

PRAISES SENATOR WRIGHT

THAT... THAT SOUNDS *JUST* LIKE STEVE. JUST LIKE HIM.

VOICES CAN BE FAKED.

IT'S THE SKULL... IT'S *GOT* TO BE.

WE *KNEW* SOMETHING ABOUT SENATOR WRIGHT WASN'T ON THE LEVEL.

BUT MAYBE HE'S NOT JUST A PATSY, HUNH?

MAYBE *HE'S* OUR LINK...FROM KRONAS TO THE RED SKULL...

AISES SE... WRIGHT

7:19 p ES

...TO THIS *OTHER* CAPTAIN AMERICA.

IF YOU'RE *SMART*...YOU'LL JUST STOP RIGHT HERE, SHARON.

TOO BAD FOR *YOU* THEN, SIN...

AH!

...THAT I'M *WAY PAST STUPID* FROM WHAT YOU PEOPLE HAVE *DONE* TO ME.

YOU'RE *NEVER* GETTING OUT OF HERE. NOT EVEN WITH ME AS *HOSTAGE.*

MY FATHER'S GOING TO PEEL THE FLESH FROM YOUR BONES.

NOT *TONIGHT,* HE WON'T...HE AND HIS *LACKEYS* ARE BUSY.

TOO *BUSY* TO *SAVE* YOU...

"...THE GIRL WHO WASN'T EVEN *INVITED* TO THE BIG EVENT."

IT'S *PERFECT,* ZOLA...

YES... I *MUST* AGREE.

HOW MANY SATELLITES HAVE YOU *COMMANDEERED* FOR THIS SCREENING, DOCTOR?

WORRY ABOUT *YOUR* PATIENT, DOCTOR... NOT *MY* CAPABILITIES.

I WAS *TRYING* TO GIVE HIM A COMPLIMENT...

LEAVE IT, *FAUSTUS...* NOTHING MATTERS BUT *THIS...*

YES...I'M PLEASED WE CONFRONTED THE *WHELP* SOONER THAN LATER.

YOU WERE *RIGHT,* ZOLA. THAT ONE *COULD* BECOME *MORE* THAN A NUISANCE...

AND WE CANNOT HAVE *THAT.*

--YOU **SEE** THAT? THIS IS **ALL** PART OF YOUR PROGRAMMING.

THAT'S IT. TWO MORE DOORS, SHARON...AND YOU'RE FREE.

JUST KEEP IGNORING THE EVIL PRINCESS...

THEY'RE **STILL** CONTROLLING YOU. I KNEW YOU WERE GOING TO DO THIS.

YOU CAN KILL HER SOME OTHER TIME.

DON'T **TEMPT** ME.

SCREW YOU.

SHUT UP.

NO. KILL ME.

KRAKK

GYAHH--

TOO SLOW...THESE DRUGS THEY'VE HAD ME ON...

WHUUU...

THAT'S RIGHT...

WOOO! WOOO! WOOO

YOU NEEDED ME FOR THE VOICE SCANNERS ON THE EXITS.

YOU WERE NEVER GONNA CUT MY THROAT.

YOU DON'T HAVE IT IN YOU!

KRAKK

I'VE GOT MORE IN ME THAN YOU CAN HANDLE, KID.

WE'LL SEE...

HANDS WHERE I CAN--

STOP. ALL OF YOU, STAY BACK.

I JUST WANTED AN AUDIENCE.

'CAUSE THIS IS MY SONG...

NO... YOU'RE **NOT** STEVE...

YOU **CAN'T** BE.

SHUT YOUR **MOUTH!**

I AM STEVE ROGERS!

THEN... DON'T YOU **KNOW** ME?

YEAH... I **KNOW** YOU...

...YOU'RE THE GUY WHO KILLED **BUCKY.**

THIS ISN'T GOOD...I'M FADING.

C'MON! YOU WERE ALL GUNG-HO!

STILL TOO MUCH OF THEIR DRUGS IN MY SYSTEM.

WASN'T PREPARED FOR A REAL FIGHT.

THOUGHT YOU WERE GONNA SCHOOL ME?!

UNH!

SMAK

I'M GOING TO LOSE.

I'M GOING TO LOSE AND THIS FREAK IS GOING TO KILL ME.

GUESS NOT, THOUGH... GUESS ALL THAT S.H.I.E.L.D. TRAINING WAS JUST A WASTE...

AND THEY'RE GOING TO TAKE MY BABY AND...AND...

NOO!

WHUDD

BUT IT LOOKS LIKE THEY DIDN'T GIVE YOU THE *FULL STORY* ON ME...

DID THEY?

NO... YOU...

THAT'S NOT...NOT RIGHT...

YOU'RE A *MURDERER*... YOU'RE NOT... YOU'RE...

WHAT IS HAPPENING, FAUSTUS?!

HE'S CRACKING...

GET HIM OUT OF THERE! BEFORE WE LOSE HIM, TOO!

SEND THE RECALL-- *NOW!*

THIS IS *NOT ON ME*... I *TOLD* YOU IT WAS TOO SOON.

LOOK... I THINK I KNOW WHO YOU ARE...

AND I CAN *HELP* YOU.

...BUT... YOU KILLED BUCKY...

...YOU KILLED HIM...

I KNOW... AND I'M SORRY...

BEEEEEEPZZZZ

UNH...

SORRY?

HEY, JUST LISTEN TO ME...

YOU'RE SORRY?!

YOU SHOULD BE DEAD!!

NO! IDIOT!

...THAT CRAZY FOOL CAN LEAD US TO THE RED SKULL.

YOUR BIRD'S FOLLOWING HIM?

A LOT OF BIRDS ARE, YEAH.

WAIT--YOU KNEW WHO HE WAS? THE CAP FROM THE NINETEEN-FIFTIES?

I HAD SUSPICIONS.

BUT I KNEW YOU'D GO OFF THE HANDLE, AND FIND OUT FOR SURE.

I...I DIDN'T MEAN TO...

MAKES YOU FEEL ANY BETTER...I THINK STEVE WOULD'VE ON THIS ONE, TOO.

NO, IT DOESN'T... 'CAUSE THAT GUY WASN'T JUST CRAZY...

HE WAS RIGHT...I DESERVE HIS HATE.

NO...THIS CANNOT BE...

SHE... SHE WAS TRYING TO KILL ME...TO ESCAPE...

GET HER TO MY MEDICAL BAY--NOW!

YOU STUPID, STUPID GIRL!

SLAPP

YOU HAVE NO IDEA WHAT YOU'VE DONE TO ME. I SHOULD NEVER HAVE LET YOU LIVE...

SO THAT'S WHAT? TWO HUNDRED AN' FIFTY DOLLARS I OWE YOU NOW?

DOLLARS? NO WAY, SAM... WE'RE PLAYING FOR EUROS.

I READ THE PAPERS, Y'KNOW.

EUROS? YOU OUGHTA BE ASHAMED OF YOURSELF.

SOME CAPTAIN AMERICA YOU'RE GONNA MAKE.

I'M A REALIST, SAM. AND IT'S A CAPITALIST WORLD.

WELL, EITHER WAY, I STILL SAY YOU CHEAT.

NO. I'M JUST GOOD. IT'S SOMETHING YOU EITHER--

HOLD ON.

WHAT?

WHAT'S HE DOING?

"HIM? SAME AS HE'S BEEN DOING THE PAST *FOUR DAYS.*"

"WHOLE LOTTA NOTHING."

"HIDING OUT AND LOOKING CONFUSED."

IT'S NOT THE *FAKE STEVE* THAT'S GOT REDWING'S ATTENTION, THOUGH.

"IT'S THE *A.I.M.* TACTICAL SQUAD CIRCLING ON HIS POSITION."

DAMN IT.

WHAT?

YOU *KNOW* WHAT.

HE'S ON THE RUN.

"HE'S TRYING TO GET *AWAY* FROM THE SKULL AND HIS PEOPLE."

WE SHOULD BE *HELPING* HIM, NOT...

USING HIM?

YEAH... I'M NOT REAL BIG ON THAT.

"I DON'T LIKE IT MUCH, EITHER, BUCK.

"BUT THE RED SKULL DOESN'T LEAVE MANY BREAD CRUMBS..."

"...AND WE CAN'T AFFORD TO WASTE THE *ONE CHANCE* WE HAVE."

WE'LL TRY TO *SAVE HIM* LATER...BUT I'M WARNING YOU...

"...THIS GUY WAS *CRAZY* LONG BEFORE DR. FAUSTUS GOT HIS HANDS ON HIM..."

"...SO THERE MAY NOT BE MUCH WE CAN DO."

YIEEEAAAA!

THIS IS A.I.M. FIELD TEAM SEVEN REPORTING IN...

WE HAVE CAPTURED THE FLAG.

GOOD. TRANSPORT HIM TO HOME BASE... STEALTH PROTOCOL.

AND THERE IS *ANOTHER* OF FAUSTUS'S MISTAKES CLEANED UP, HERR SKULL.

IN THE *OLD DAYS*, YOU WOULD NOT HAVE *STOOD* FOR THIS.

WE ARE NOT *IN* THE OLD DAYS, DOCTOR ZOLA.

AND IN SPITE OF HIS *OVERBLOWN EGO*, IT WAS FAUSTUS'S CONTROL OF *THE GIRL* WHICH ALLOWED THIS *ALL* TO HAPPEN.

IF ONLY SHE WERE *STILL* OF USE TO US.

WE NEED HER FOR *ONE* THING, YET, IF YOU'RE SERIOUS, WHICH I HOPE YOU ARE *NOT*.

I AM STILL CONSTRUCTING THE PLATFORM, FOR ONE, AND--

MY INSOLENT *DAUGHTER* HAS LEFT ME NO OTHER CHOICE.

OR WOULD YOU...WOULD YOU HAVE ME...

...GAHH...
WOULD YOU
HAVE *US*...

...STUCK
LIKE *THIS*
FOREVER?

INDEED,
NO, HERR LUKIN...
I WOULD
NOT.

THEN
YOU'LL GET
IT *READY*, ZOLA...
AND YOU'LL
FIX US.

OR YOUR
LEADER AND
I WILL *BOTH*
GO INSANE.

WHICHEVER
PART OF DOOM'S
DEVICE STILL
ELUDES YOUR
GRASP...FIGURE
IT OUT.

AND GET
IT DONE
NOW...

...BEFORE
ANYTHING
ELSE GOES
WRONG.

IT'S ALL GONE SO BADLY FOR *YOU*, MY DEAR... I FEEL AT LEAST PARTLY TO BLAME.

PARTLY?

YOU BROUGHT ME HERE! YOU SON OF A--

HUSH.

CALM YOURSELF.

THAT'S IT... *YES*...THERE'S STILL A PIECE OF *MY* AGENT 13 LEFT.

NOW *LISTEN*...

...YOU'VE LOST YOUR BABY, SHARON, AND THAT'S *ANGERED* THE SKULL.

I'M SURE IT HAS.

BECAUSE YOU KNEW THEY WERE *NEVER* GOING TO LET YOU KEEP IT, *DIDN'T YOU?*

DID *YOU* INTEND TO DIE AS WELL?

MANY TIMES, DOCTOR... YES.

ANYTHING TO KEEP IT SAFE...AND AWAY FROM *HIM*.

I SEE... AND RIGHT *YOU* ARE. I WOULD RATHER SEE ANYTHING I CARED ABOUT *DEAD* THAN IN THE HANDS OF THOSE *MADMEN.*

YOU'RE TRULY A *REMARKABLE SPECIMEN,* AGENT 13... TRULY.

I HOPE THAT YOU MAKE IT THROUGH THE COMING DAYS...

BECAUSE THEY *STILL* NEED YOU... YOU ARE THE *CONSTANT.*

I DON'T UNDERSTAND...

YOU WILL... ALTHOUGH I WON'T BE HERE TO SEE IT.

BUT I LEAVE YOU WITH TWO GIFTS...YOUR S.H.I.E.L.D. *GPS* TRANSMITTER.

AND THIS...

...*FORGET* YOUR GRIEF.

YOU WERE *NEVER* PREGNANT. IT WAS ALL A BAD DREAM.

YOU'LL HAVE *CONTROL* OF YOUR MIND AGAIN WHEN I'M GONE...USE IT WISELY.

YOU'LL HAVE TO BE *STRONG* TO SURVIVE, SHARON.

THIS IS *CRAZY*, SAM...

...THERE'S NO WAY A.I.M. HAS AN UNDERGROUND BASE IN *ALBANY*...

IT'S THE STATE *CAPITAL*, FOR CRYIN' OUT LOUD.

NO ONE'S SAYING IT'S AN A.I.M. BASE, JUST THAT'S WHERE THE *BIRDS* SAY THEY TOOK THE FAKE STEVE.

COULD BE SOME *KRONAS* HOLDING...THEY'VE GOT THEIR HOOKS INTO SO MANY POLITICIANS, PROBABLY WANT TO KEEP THEM CLOSE.

COULD FIND OUT REAL QUICK IF YOU'D LET ME CALL S.H.I.E.L.D. IN ON THIS.

NO WAY, SAM...I DON'T WANNA CAUSE NATALIA ANY MORE--

--TROUBLE...

HELLO, BOYS.

I WAS HOPING TO RUN INTO YOU.

NATALIA... WHAT ARE YOU--

HOW DID YOU FIND US? SAM?

NOT ME, PARTNER...

WE'RE OPERATING ON A TIP, ACTUALLY, FROM A DISGRUNTLED MINION WHO INFORMED US YOU MIGHT BE ON THIS TRAIL, TOO.

IT APPEARS THAT THE RED SKULL AND HIS PEOPLE HAVE A BASE IN--

ALBANY... YEAH, WE KNOW.

WELL, WHAT YOU DON'T KNOW IS THAT AGENT 13'S *GPS TRANSMITTER* WENT LIVE LAST NIGHT...

AND WE'VE BEEN CASING THE FACILITY ALL DAY. IT'S *NOT* A TRAP.

DISGRUNTLED *MINION*, HUH?

IT APPEARS DR. FAUSTUS HAS DECIDED TO *END* THEIR PARTNERSHIP...

WITHOUT *INFORMING* THE SKULL, OF COURSE.

SO, WHY COME BACK FOR *US?* I THOUGHT I WAS *PERSONA NON GRATA* AT S.H.I.E.L.D...

WHAT *AREN'T* YOU SAYING?

FAUSTUS DIDN'T *ONLY* GIVE US THE LOCATION OF THE SECRET BASE, JAMES.

HE ALSO REMINDED US SOMETHING *ELSE* IS HAPPENING IN ALBANY TODAY...

WHAT?

A PART OF THE RED SKULL'S PLAN WHICH *CAPTAIN AMERICA* IS GOING TO STOP.

"...THE MAN ON YOUR LEFT WILL FALL."

--SINCE **ROSS PEROT** THAT AN **INDEPENDENT CANDIDATE** HAS BEEN INVITED TO BE PART OF ANY PRESIDENTIAL DEBATES. AND YET THERE'S --

"THEN YOU WILL DIVE TO SAVE THE MAN ON YOUR RIGHT."

--SENATOR WRIGHT'S POPULARITY IN THE POLLS, THE COMMITTEE HAD LITTLE CHOICE.

AND AS YOU CAN SEE, TURNOUT IS **MASSIVE.** ALREADY THE HALL IS FILLED TO--

DO YOU UNDERSTAND ME, SIN?

OF COURSE, FATHER. I'M NOT AN IDIOT.

THIS IS YOUR CHANCE TO PROVE THAT TO ME.

SENATOR WRIGHT IS TO BE WOUNDED ONLY.

UNDERSTOOD, FATHER.

I'VE BEEN **TOLERANT** OF YOU, BUT DON'T DISAPPOINT ME AGAIN, GIRL.

HERR SKULL?

WHAT?

WE HAVE THE SUBJECT. WHAT DO YOU WANT US TO DO WITH HIM, SIR?

AH, GOOD...

PUT HIM IN THE IMMERSION ROOM...

...AND SOMEONE INFORM DR. FAUSTUS HIS PATIENT HAS RETURNED FOR FURTHER EDUCATION.

YES, SIR.

IF I'D HAD MORE TIME WITH IT... I COULD HAVE UNRAVELED ITS SECRETS...

NOW GO, GET THE GIRL...

AND NONE OF YOUR UNDERLINGS ARE TO KNOW WHAT WE DO HERE.

OF COURSE, HERR SKULL.

ANOTHER TIME, YOU WILL...

...BUT FOR NOW, THE PURPOSE I ALWAYS INTENDED IS MORE THAN ENOUGH.

SIR...?

WHAT IS IT?

IT'S... MAYBE A PROBLEM...

WE CAN'T FIND DR. FAUSTUS, SIR...

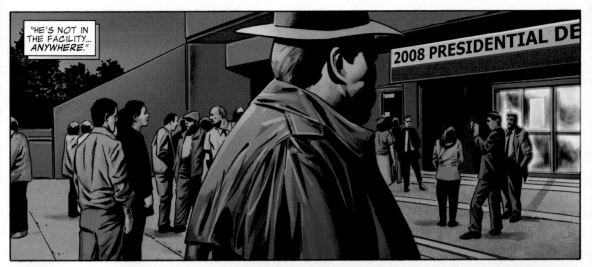

"HE'S NOT IN THE FACILITY... ANYWHERE."

2008 PRESIDENTIAL DE

AND IF YOU'LL ALL PLEASE TAKE YOUR SEATS, WE CAN BRING OUT THE CANDIDATES FOR THIS HISTORIC FIRST PRESIDENTIAL DEBATE OF 2008.

CLAP CLAP CLAP

CLAP CLAP CLAP

...SUCH A WASTE...

AND WHAT OF YOU? HAVE YOU SEEN FAUSTUS, GIRL?

NO, WHY?

NEVER MIND, YOU. JUST MOVE.

WE HAVE NEED OF YOUR PATHETIC FRAME AGAIN.

OW--STOP PULLING.

TNNK

KNNK

WHAT IN THE NAME OF--

BOOM

CLAP CLAP CLAP

CLAP CLAP CLAP

THANK YOU...YES... BUT WHAT THE SENATOR'S *RHETORIC* FAILS TO GRASP IS—

—THAT CHANGE HAS A *PRICE.* AND WHO IS IT THAT WILL PAY THAT BILL, I'D ASK HIM?

GAHH... YES, FATHER... UNDERSTOOD, FATHER...

SO WEAK... WEAK...

WEAK... LITTLE... LITTLE GIRL...

WELL... THE HELL WITH *YOU,* FATHER.

I DON'T WANT TO BE HERE.

KRAK

I WANT TO BE WITH SAM AND NATALIA, ON THE HUNT...

WA-RING

I WANT TO BE BASHING THE RED SKULL'S TEETH IN...

NO! NO WAY!

...AND SAVING STEVE'S GIRL.

GET THE CANDIDATES CLEAR!

I CAN HANDLE THIS!

BUT DAMN IT, NATALIA WAS RIGHT...

WHO THE HELL ARE YOU?!

WHAT DOES IT LOOK LIKE?

THE SKULL'S DAUGHTER IS SLIPPERY...

NYAHH!

KRAKK

...AND HER BACKUP ARE WELL-TRAINED.

BUT THERE'S NO WAY I'M FAILING... NOT TODAY.

BUDDA BUDDA BUDDA

THIS MUST BE HOW STEVE FELT. THIS UNIFORM...IT CARRIES A WEIGHT, BUT IT'S NOT A BURDEN...

BUDDA BUDDA BUDDA

THIS WILL HURT, GIRL.

WHAT...?

BZOWW

UHNN--

HELP ME GET HER HOOKED IN.

YES, AND QUICKLY, ZOLA... WE HAVE LITTLE TIME TO SPARE.

THEN PERHAPS IT WOULD HAVE BEEN BEST IF YOU HADN'T DECIDED TO BRING THE ENTIRE COMPLEX DOWN AROUND US.

OLD HABITS, DOCTOR...THEY DIE HARDER THAN I DO.

AND I DON'T INTEND TO BE TRAPPED BY MY ENEMIES...OR IN THIS BODY ANY LONGER...

NOW *DO* IT, DAMN YOU.

IT HAS ALREADY BEGUN, HERR SKULL.

WHAT...? WAIT. WHAT DID THEY...?

OW. NEEDLES?

OW.

SHE'S *WAKING UP* ALREADY!

IT DOESN'T *MATTER.* IT'S ALREADY BEEN *LOCKED...*

OR *UNLOCKED...* PERHAPS THAT'S A BETTER WORD.

WHAT ARE THESE MANIACS...NO...

WHAT ARE THEY DOING TO ME *NOW?*

WASTING TOO MUCH TIME ON THE UNDERLINGS.

BUT I CAN'T TAKE THE RISK OF ANYONE CONFUSING THEM WITH ACTUAL SECURITY.

AAAHH!

WHERE IS SIN? SHE CAN'T JUST BE RUNNING.

WHAMM

THAT'S WAY TOO EASY...

...AND SHE'S WAY TOO PSYCHO.

AH, ROCKET-PROPELLED GRENADES... AS DEVILISH AS ALWAYS, FATHER...

BUDDY-- MOVE THAT TRUCK!

OR WE'LL MOVE IT FOR YOU-- NOW!

WHAT...WHAT IS THIS...?

WHAT AM I SEEING?

SOMETHING ALIVE? WHAT IS...IS IT GROWING...?

NO. IT'S NOT... IT'S...

IS THAT MY... IS THAT...

NO.

ZOLA. WHAT IS SHE--

NO!

FRAZZZAAATTZZ

GET DOWN!

KA-FRATTZZ

NO... WHAT DID SHE *DO?*

SHE BROKE THE CONNECTION, WHICH SHORTED-OUT THE DEVICE.

I COULD REPAIR IT, BUT THERE'S NO TIME. THEY'LL BE HERE SOON.

SHE'S HERE SOMEWHERE, BUCK... JUST FOLLOW YOUR GUT.

WHAT DOES SHE WANT? WHAT'S HER AGENDA?

OH GOD... NO.

NO!

TOO LATE, CAPTAIN ASSHAT.

DLEET

SHE'S NOT HERE, NATASHA. THERE'S NO SIGN OF HER.

HOLD ON... WAIT...

AH, DAMN IT.

A GPS TRACKER...BUT NO SHARON CARTER.

SO THEN, WHERE THE HELL *IS* SHE?

HOW LONG WAS I OUT...*FIVE MINUTES?* HAVE TO KEEP MOVING...

MOVE THROUGH THE PAIN...CAN'T LET HIM...

CAN'T LET THE RED SKULL GET AWAY...

...NOT WITH ALL HE'S DONE...

...BUT...
BUT...BUT...
I WAS...BUT...
I...
...

OKAY...GOOD
ENOUGH...

...I'M
DONE
NOW...

OH, I AM
AFRAID YOU HAVE
NO CONCEPT, GIRL...
OF HOW FUTILE...
HOW UTTERLY
FUTILE...

AAAIIEEEEEE-- SKKRAAZZZ

FASCIST FREAK... PSYCHO...

PLEASE TELL ME... YOU...YOU'RE...

...ONE OF... THE GOOD GUYS NOW...

...RIGHT...?

RIGHT--STUPIDEST THING I'VE EVER DONE? NOT QUITE, BUT CLOSE.

PHWOOOM

I HOPE STARK WASN'T KIDDING ABOUT THE IMPACT-RESISTANCE ON THIS SUIT...

KRA-KOOM

UHNN--

SKAASHH

OKAY... AT LEAST I SURVIVED...

...OW...

...EXACTLY ACCORDING TO MY HALF-ASSED PLAN...

AGENTS-- STAND CLEAR!

ON MY MARK!

...SORT OF.

UH...JUST HOLD ON A...A SECOND...

YELLOW DOG 2, REPORT?

SHOOTER IS *DOWN*, SIR.

REPEAT... SHOOTER IS *DOWN*.

ALL RIGHT, PEOPLE... WEAPONS *DOWN*.

WHAT...? WHAT'RE *YOU*...?

NICE WORK, CAP...

GOOD SAVE.

HEY, CAP--OVER *HERE!*

HEY, CAP!

WAY TO GO, CAP! *YEAH!*

HEY, CAP-- CAN WE GET A *STATEMENT?!*

--RUN THE CAPTAIN AMERICA *BLOG*--

--A PICTURE FOR MY WIFE, CAP?!

OVER HERE, CAP-- *SMILE!*

FOR A SECOND, I REMEMBER WHEN IT USED TO BE LIKE THIS ALL THE TIME. THE SOLDIERS CHEERING ON ME AND STEVE.

AND FOR A SECOND, IT DOESN'T SEEM THAT LONG AGO...

...FOR JUST A SECOND.

SHE STILL *BREATHING?*

YES. SHE'S TAKEN SOME *PUNISHMENT...* BUT SHE'S STILL WITH US.

LOOK AT THIS...ARNIM ZOLA *AND* THE RED SKULL?

SHARON DID *ALL* THIS?

I WOULDN'T PUT IT *PAST* HER...SHE'S ALWAYS IMPRESSED ME.

...SAM...?

EASY, SHARON... TAKE IT SLOW...

OH SAM... I DID IT...

I *KILLED* STEVE...I DIDN'T MEAN TO... BUT...

IT'S *OKAY,* SHARON...WE KNOW...

THEY WERE *CONTROLLING* YOU...BUT IT'S ALL OVER NOW... IT'S OVER...

...THE GOOD GUYS WON...

--AND MY PERSONAL PHYSICIAN HAS CONFIRMED IT...

...SHARON HAD A *MISCARRIAGE* A LITTLE OVER A WEEK AGO.

THE SCAR ON HER STOMACH IS FROM THE ATTACK THAT *CAUSED* THE MISCARRIAGE.

AND SHE *DOESN'T REMEMBER?* SHE DOESN'T REMEMBER BEING *PREGNANT?*

Epilogue One

Two Days Later-- The S.H.I.E.L.D. Helicarrier

IT'S INSANE, BUT...DR. FAUSTUS *TURNED* ON THE RED SKULL IN THE END...

MAYBE HE THOUGHT HE WAS *HELPING* HER?

THE QUESTION IS, WHAT HAPPENS NOW? SHE *DESERVES* TO KNOW...BUT I CAN'T BRING MYSELF TO DO IT.

YEAH, I HEAR YOU. TELL YOU *WHAT*...

I'M GONNA TAKE CARE OF SHARON FOR A WHILE...I THINK STEVE WOULD *WANT* THAT.

AND WHEN SHE'S *STRONG ENOUGH* TO KNOW THE TRUTH...I'LL TELL HER...

...BUT NOT TODAY.

--LISTEN TO ME CLOSELY, SENATOR, AND YOU *MAY* SURVIVE WITH YOUR PENSION.

BUT IT'S NOT *FAIR*...I WASN'T *RESPONSIBLE.*

HOW COULD I *KNOW?* HOW--

IF IT WERE *JUST* DOCTOR FAUSTUS *USING YOU*, THAT WOULD BE *BAD* ENOUGH...

...BUT YOU WERE *DEEP* IN THE POCKET OF *KRONAS* LONG BEFORE THAT, SENATOR WRIGHT...

BUT...I WASN'T...

YOU WERE *RIPE* FOR THE PICKING, IS WHAT YOU WERE.

SO YOU CAN EITHER RESIGN *AND* WITHDRAW FROM THE ELECTION... OR YOU CAN BE PUBLICLY BRANDED A *TRAITOR...*

...FOREVER LINKED TO A CORPORATION THAT WAS FRONTING *DOMESTIC TERRORISM.*

IT'S *YOUR* CHOICE.

--REGRET TO INFORM MY SUPPORTERS THAT I'M *WITHDRAWING* FROM THE PRESIDENTIAL RACE, AND RESIGNING MY SEAT IN THE SENATE.

THE ACTIONS OF MY *SECURITY TEAM,* WORKING UNDER ORDERS FROM--

YOU'RE *GOOD,* NATALIA. DID HE EVEN *BLINK?*

OF COURSE NOT.

OH, *LOOK...*

KRONAS CORP. SCANDAL SEN. WRIGHT RESIGNS

11:04 p

...THEY'RE PLAYING IT *AGAIN...*

--AND WERE ALL SAVED BY THE ACTIONS OF THE *NEW* CAPTAIN AMERICA. OUR OVERNIGHT POLLING SHOWS--

NEW CAPTAIN AMERICA SAVES PRES. CANDIDATES

11:05 p

UGH...NO MORE...

CLIK

PLEASE, YOU'RE A *STAR,* JAMES...THE PEOPLE *LOVE YOU...*

ENJOY IT WHILE IT *LASTS...*

I'M *TRYING,* BUT...I JUST CAN'T STOP THINKING HOW *CLOSE* HE CAME, THE RED SKULL...

HE ALMOST HAD HIS OWN *PRESIDENT.*

--SOMEDAY YOU WILL **SEE**, AND THEN YOU WILL FORGIVE ME, MASTER... I AM CERTAIN OF THAT.

THERE WAS SIMPLY NO OTHER CHOICE... NO TIME FOR OPTIONS.

BUT I PROMISE YOU IT IS ONLY TEMPORARY.

I KNOW WE HAVE HAD OUR **DIFFERENCES**, HERR SKULL...BUT ARNIM ZOLA REMAINS LOYAL TO HIS **OATHS**, AS ALWAYS...

...AND I **SWEAR** I WILL BE BACK FOR YOU SOON...AND I WILL **FIX** THIS.

NO...NO... NO...